On the Brink of Extinction

Extinction
The California Condor

ON THE BRINK

OF EXTINCTION

THE CALIFORNIA CONDOR

BY CAROLINE ARNOLD

Photographs by
MICHAEL WALLACE

A GULLIVER GREEN BOOK
HARCOURT BRACE JOVANOVICH,
PUBLISHERS
San Diego New York London

HBJ

Text copyright © 1993 by Caroline Arnold
Photographs copyright © 1993 by Greater Los Angeles Zoo Association Condor Fund

Library of Congress Cataloging-in-Publication Data
Arnold, Caroline.
On the brink of extinction: the California condor/by Caroline
Arnold; photographs by Michael Wallace. — 1st ed.
p.   cm.
"Gulliver books"
Summary: Describes the history of the condor in North America and
the efforts to capture and breed the few remaining California
condors to save them from extinction.
ISBN 0-15-257990-7 (hc.) — ISBN 0-15-257991-5 (pbk.)
1. California condor — North America — Juvenile literature.   2. Rare birds — North
America — Juvenile literature.   3. Endangered species — North America — Juvenile
literature.   4. Wildlife conservation — North America — Juvenile literature.
[1. California condor.   2. Condors.   3. Rare birds.   4. Wildlife conservation.]
I. Wallace, Michael Phillip, ill.   II. Title.
QL696.F33A76   1993
598.9'12 — dc20   92-14914

Designed by Lisa Peters
Printed and bound by Tien Wah Press, Singapore

BCDE   ABCDE (pbk.)

Printed in Singapore

All photographs are by Michael Wallace with the following exceptions:
Dr. Noel Snyder, back jacket, pp. 5, 15 (left); Jesse Grantham, pp. 13 (top left), 42;
Helen Snyder, p. 13 (bottom); David Clendennen, pp. 15 (right), 45;
Allison Leete, p. 23; Robert Mesta, p. 38.

ACKNOWLEDGMENTS

I WANT TO THANK Dr. Michael Wallace, Curator of Birds and Director of the Condor Program at the Los Angeles Zoo for his willingness to cooperate on this project, for his expert advice and careful reading of the manuscript, and for his excellent photography. For their contribution of additional photos we are both grateful to photographers Helen Snyder, Dr. Noel Snyder, David Clendennen, Allison Leete, Robert Mesta, and Jesse Grantham.

Many people have contributed to the effort to save the California condors. Staff and volunteers at both the Los Angeles Zoo and the San Diego Wild Animal Park have played a critical role in the captive breeding of condors along with the U.S. Fish and Wildlife Service Team, which oversees the care of the condors in the field. The California Condor Recovery Team, headed by Lloyd Kiff, includes representatives of the U.S. Fish and Wildlife Service, the U.S. Forest Service, the U.S. Bureau of Land Management, the California Department of Fish and Game, both zoos mentioned above, and members of the academic community. Without the enthusiasm and dedication of all these people and many more, there might be a very different condor story to tell.

In April 1987, on a remote mountainside in southern California, a group of scientists watched anxiously as AC-9, the last of the free-flying California condors, circled overhead. Gliding gracefully on giant wings, the huge bird eyed the fresh carcass that lay in the clearing. Like other vultures, it depended on finding dead animals for its food. Finally AC-9 landed and cautiously approached the meat. Before the bird had time to escape, the scientists released their net and caught it. One person rushed forward to grab the condor and safely untangle it while another brought over a small carrier in which they would transport the bird to the zoo. AC-9 and the twenty-six other condors already in captivity were the only California condors left in the world. If they died, their species would become extinct. The scientists hoped that placing these birds together in male-female pairs would lead to successful breeding in zoos. After a few years, young condors could be returned to the wild to begin a new healthy flock.

AC-9 soars overhead.

FOR FORTY THOUSAND YEARS or more, California condors ranged across much of North America. They fed on the carcasses of giant sloths, mastodons, and other large mammals that roamed the continent during the last Ice Age. When these animals became extinct about ten thousand years ago, the condors disappeared everywhere except along the west coast, where they ate fish and other sea animals that washed up on the beach. Native Americans who lived in the area knew condors well and depicted them in their art. In the early 1800s, condors ranged from what is now Baja California to present-day British Columbia.

A full-grown California condor has a wingspan of nearly ten feet and can weigh as much as 23½ pounds. It is the largest flying land bird in North America. The scientific name of the California condor, *Gymnogyps californianus,* comes from the Greek words *gymnos,* meaning "naked," and *gyps,* meaning "vulture." Like most other vultures, the condor has few feathers on its head or neck. Probing for meat in a bloody carcass can be messy, and the absence of feathers makes it easier for a vulture to keep clean. The skin on the condor's neck varies in color depending on the bird's age. Birds under four years old have dark heads. The skin on an adult condor's head varies from cream to yellow and can look almost orange during the breeding season. On its body, the condor's feathers are coal black except for a row of white feathers under the wings. On its neck, a ring of black plumes creates the effect of an elegant boa.

The holes on either side of the condor's head are its ears.

THE SLIGHTLY LARGER Andean condor from South America is closely related to the California condor. Soaring above high mountain ridges, coastal plains, and along the seashore, the Andean condor ranges from Venezuela in the north to Tierra del Fuego in the south. Our word "condor" comes from *kúntur,* the Quechua word used for the condor by the Incan people in South America.

The Andean condor has a wingspan of ten feet, and with a weight of up to thirty-three pounds, it is the largest of all flying birds. An adult Andean condor has a black, red, or yellow head, a white collar around its neck, a black body and tail feathers, and several rows of large white feathers along the top of its wings. Young birds are brown with dark heads. Although the Andean condor is also endangered, it still flies freely over much of its range and provides a good opportunity for people to observe condor behavior in the wild. In North America, Andean condors have helped scientists to develop and test techniques both for breeding condors in captivity and for putting birds back into the wild.

LEFT: *The male Andean condor is somewhat larger than the female and has a large fleshy knob called a caruncle on its head.*

ABOVE: *An Andean condor soars over southern California mountains.*

11

As SETTLERS BUILT FARMS and ranches in the American west, the California condors started to disappear. They were shot for sport and for museum exhibits and also died after eating poisons put out for coyotes. Some birds had difficulty breeding when their nest areas were disturbed by egg collectors or when land nearby was developed for human use. By the early twentieth century, condors lived only in the rugged mountains and foothills north of Los Angeles and at the southern end of the San Joaquin Valley in central California.

In the mid-1940s, farmers began using a new pesticide, DDT. When birds eat food contaminated by DDT, the chemicals accumulate in their bodies and eventually cause them to produce eggs with shells so damaged that they break when the parent birds sit on them. Although the use of DDT was banned in 1974, traces of it still remain in the environment. Other continuing problems for condors include further reduction of their habitat, accidents caused by collisions with power lines, and slow poisoning from eating lead bullets in the carcasses of animals shot by hunters.

In 1973, the United States Congress passed the Endangered Species Act to protect animals such as the condor. Shortly after that, they brought together representatives from several government agencies and the National Audubon Society to form the California Condor Recovery Team. This group developed a number of plans, which included studying the birds both in the wild and in captivity, trying to make the natural environment safer for condors, and educating the public.

TOP LEFT: *Adult condor that died from lead poisoning*

TOP RIGHT: *X-ray of another condor showing shotgun pellets embedded in its body*

BOTTOM: *Condor eggshell damaged from the effects of DDT*

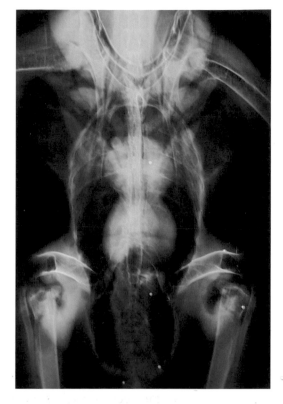

BELOW: *The large numbers on condor tags can be read easily, even at a distance.*

TOP LEFT: *Wild California condor at entrance to nest area*

TOP RIGHT: *The female condor lays a single egg on the dirt or sand floor of the nest cave.*

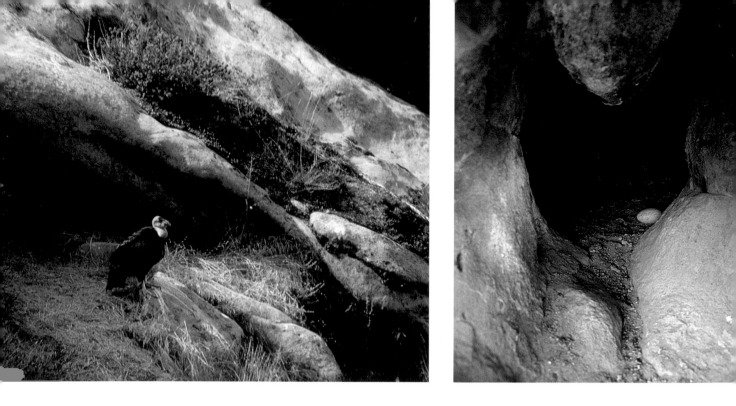

WHEN STUDYING THE CONDORS in the wild, scientists needed to be able to identify individual birds. After testing tagging methods on Andean condors, many of the California condors were caught and marked with light-weight tags on their wings. (AC-9, for instance, stood for adult condor number nine.) When a bird was tagged, it could also be weighed and measured and given a health exam.

The condor population was shrinking because birds were dying faster than they could be replaced. Condors do not begin to breed until they are six or seven years old, and a pair usually lays only one egg a season. Because condor parents frequently care for their chick longer than a year, they often produce a new youngster only every other year. Even under good conditions, only some of the condor eggs laid each year hatch successfully. They may be infertile, or the chick inside may fail to develop properly. In the wild, eggs also might be destroyed by predators such as ravens.

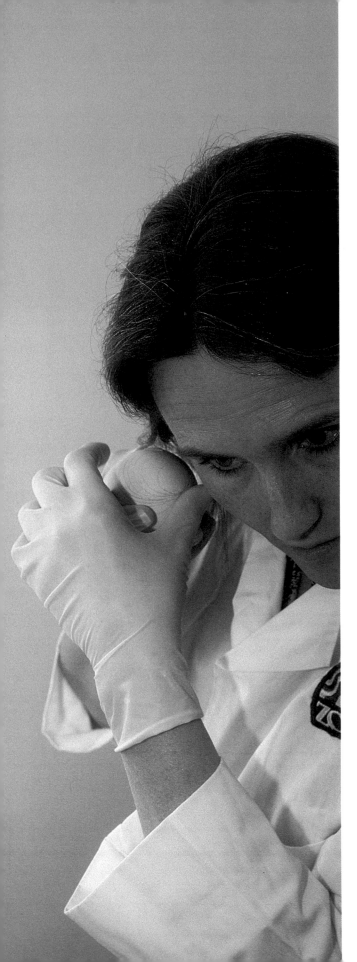

FROM THEIR EXPERIENCE with captive Andean condors, scientists knew that if a pair had their first egg of the season removed, they often would mate again and produce a second egg. In some cases, if this were also taken away, the birds would lay a third egg. Those eggs removed from the condor nests could be hatched in an incubator, and the chicks could then be raised by people. Raising the birds in captivity would assure their safety, and the number of chicks could be dramatically increased. This way, a condor pair could produce up to six chicks in two years, whereas a pair in the wild would usually rear only one during that same period.

Between 1982 and 1986, a number of eggs were removed from wild nests and successfully hatched at the San Diego Zoo. Some young condors were also trapped and brought to the Los Angeles Zoo in hopes that when they matured they would mate and produce additional chicks. In the early 1980s there were still five healthy breeding pairs in the wild. Zoo-raised chicks could help the total population to increase more rapidly.

LEFT: *Zoo staff check each condor egg daily.*

RIGHT: *Condor-shaped puppets imitate the actions of parent birds.*

Unfortunately, the number of wild condors continued to shrink, and by 1986 there was only one breeding pair left. Scientists decided, after much discussion, to bring the remaining wild birds into zoos before they, too, disappeared. As soon as enough chicks were produced to assure the safety of the captive flock, some of the young condors could go back to the wild. Andean condor chicks raised in captivity and then taken back to their native habitat showed that captive-bred condor chicks could be returned to the wild successfully if they were not allowed to become tame.

California condor breeding areas were built at the San Diego Wild Animal Park and at the Los Angeles Zoo in California. Each facility has an office, a food preparation area, buildings for incubating eggs and feeding young chicks, and large flight cages for the older birds. In the breeding pens, each cage is home to one male and one female bird. The cage is large enough to allow the condors to fly and has several perches as well as a pond for drinking and bathing. At one end there is an enclosed nest box and a sheltered place for roosting. At the other, a screened area called a "blind" allows people to watch the condors without being seen by the birds.

ABOVE: *The breeding cages were built in areas closed to the public so the birds would be disturbed as little as possible.*

RIGHT: *One perch in each enclosure is also a scale; caretakers can use binoculars to read the condor's weight. Weight is a good measure of a bird's health.*

18

In the wild, condors form pairs naturally, and in most cases, once a male and female have chosen each other as mates, they remain together for the rest of their lives. One of the problems for California condors today is that with so few birds left, many of them are closely related. By keeping track of each bird and its ancestry, scientists can follow the genetic makeup of the population as it grows. At the Los Angeles Zoo and the San Diego Wild Animal Park, the male and female of each breeding pair have been carefully chosen from the least-related individuals in the flock. This helps ensure stronger offspring and will make the population more adaptable in the future.

THE CONDOR PENS at the zoo are known by the staff as the "condorminiums" and are constructed side by side so that the birds can see and hear one another. Like other vultures, condors are social birds and normally live in flocks. In the wild, condors sometimes search for food together. Keeping one another in view, members of the group fan out while flying over a large area. Using their excellent eyesight, condors scan the ground below for dead or dying animals or the activities of other scavengers that suggest food is nearby. When one condor finds food, the others note its descent and fly over to join it.

Vultures are among nature's garbage collectors. Along with other scavengers, they clean off carcasses that would otherwise rot and spoil. In the past, the usual food of wild California condors included dead cattle, sheep, ground squirrels, deer, and horses. At the zoo, the condors' diet consists of dead rats and mice, fish, and the meat of large animals such as sheep and goats. A condor has a big appetite and will eat enough at one feeding to last for two or more days.

After eating, a condor usually wipes its head in sand or grass to clean itself. It may then look for a shallow pond where it can drink and bathe. By dipping its head and wings forward, it splashes water backward over its head and body. After a few minutes in the water, the bird climbs out and finds a quiet place in the sun to rest and to clean and arrange its feathers.

LEFT: Sometimes a condor uses its foot to hold down its food while eating. Unlike a bird of prey, however, a condor cannot grasp objects with its talons.

ABOVE LEFT: A thirsty condor takes a drink.

ABOVE RIGHT: A young condor suns itself.

BEGINNING IN LATE FALL, California condors get ready to mate. As in many other species of birds, the changing day length triggers chemical changes in the birds' bodies that make it possible for them to breed. The male condor begins courtship by swaying and "dancing" in front of the female with his wings partially open. At first the female may ignore him, and if he gets too close, will peck him or push him away. Only when she is well within the breeding season will she permit the male to mate with her.

In December or January, the condor pair chooses a nest site. In the wild, a suitable nesting place is protected from the weather, is safe from predators, has a level sandy spot where the egg can rest, is large enough for both adult birds, and has nearby tree branches or rock ledges where the birds can perch. Wild condors usually nest in small caves or holes in cliffs, although they have sometimes been known to nest in large, hollow trees. At the zoo, cavelike nest boxes are built into the upper end of each flight cage. Condors do not build nests like most birds, but simply lay the egg on the sandy floor of the cave or box.

LEFT: *A male condor courts his mate.*

RIGHT: *An egg is fertile only after a successful mating.*

TRAINED OBSERVERS AT the zoo watch the condor pairs daily. Numbered tags, placed on the right wings of males and the left wings of females, help observers identify the birds. During the breeding season, the birds are also watched via video monitors. A female condor spends an increasing amount of time inside the nest box as she gets ready to produce an egg. As soon as an egg is laid, keepers carefully remove it and place it in an incubator to keep it at a specific temperature and humidity.

TOP: From behind one-way Plexiglas, researchers can study the birds without disturbing them.

BOTTOM: Closed-circuit television monitors allow observers to watch all the condor nest enclosures at once.

RIGHT: Candling a condor egg allows a peek at the developing chick.

24

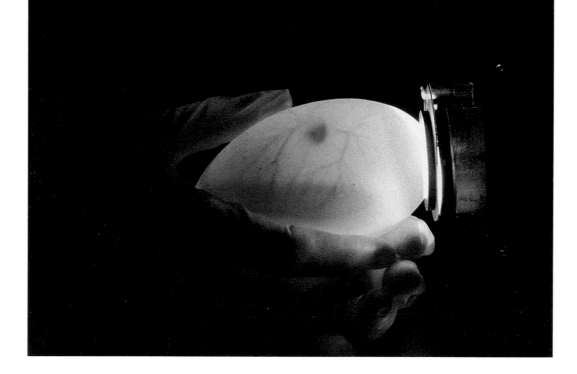

If a condor pair at the zoo lays three eggs in a season, the last egg is replaced with a dummy egg. As they would with a real egg, the condor pair takes turns sitting on it. Then after they have incubated it for a time, the keepers give the birds an Andean condor egg to hatch and raise. This allows the condors to practice being parents. In 1992, a pair of California condors that had successfully raised Andean chicks in the past was allowed to rear one of their own chicks. As the population grows, more pairs will be allowed to raise their chicks as well.

A California condor egg is about five inches long and three inches in diameter. It has a thick, pale blue shell. The condor parents use their beaks to turn their egg several times during each day, which prevents the membranes around the developing chick from sticking to one side. For the same reason, the incubator at the zoo slowly rotates the eggs.

Keepers check on the eggs' development every day by holding them up to a special bright light. This process, called "candling," reveals the dark shape of blood vessels feeding the growing chick inside. A light portion at the larger end is an air pocket. It grows bigger as the chick develops, and its changing size is marked by pencil rings around the shell.

APPROXIMATELY FIFTY-SEVEN days after it was laid, a condor egg hatches. The chick uses a hard knob, called an "egg tooth," on the top of its beak to make the first crack, which is called the "pip." Rotating its body inside the egg, the chick continues to press against the inside of the hard shell and gradually breaks free. The entire hatching process for a condor chick may take up to four days. During this time a member of the zoo staff constantly watches the egg and provides help if necessary.

ABOVE: *When the pip appears, the egg is placed in a special hatching incubator.*

TOP LEFT: *A chick pushes against the tough shell.*

TOP RIGHT: *When the circle is complete, the top of the shell pops off.*

BOTTOM: *At first, the feathers of the chick are wet from moisture inside the egg.*

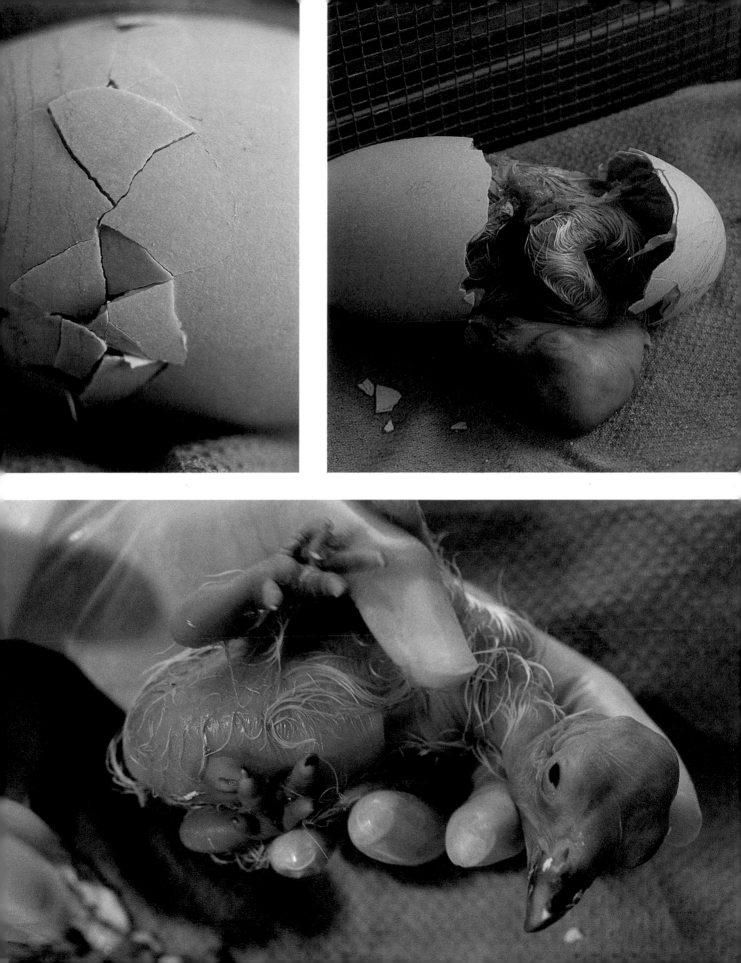

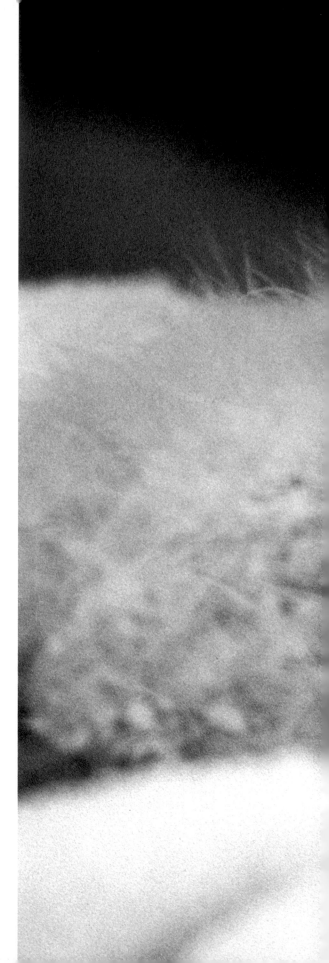

A NEWLY HATCHED chick weighs about six ounces. Although it can see and hear, it is only aware of its immediate surroundings. Within an hour or so, the chick's feathers dry out and the soft, white down helps to keep its body warm. Male and female condor chicks look alike when they are newly hatched. When the chick is about three months old, scientists take a blood sample and use it to determine the chick's sex.

The first successful hatching of a condor chick from an egg laid in captivity was at the San Diego Wild Animal Park on April 29, 1988. That chick was called Molloko, a Chumash name for the condor. The Chumash are a Native American tribe in southern California. For centuries, the Chumash and other Native Americans have told stories about condors, used their feathers and bones in special ceremonies, and held festivals and celebrations in their honor. Because the condor is an important part of their heritage, all of the California condor chicks hatched at the Los Angeles Zoo and the San Diego Wild Animal Park have been given Native American names.

The pink skin of the newly hatched condor gradually changes to gray.

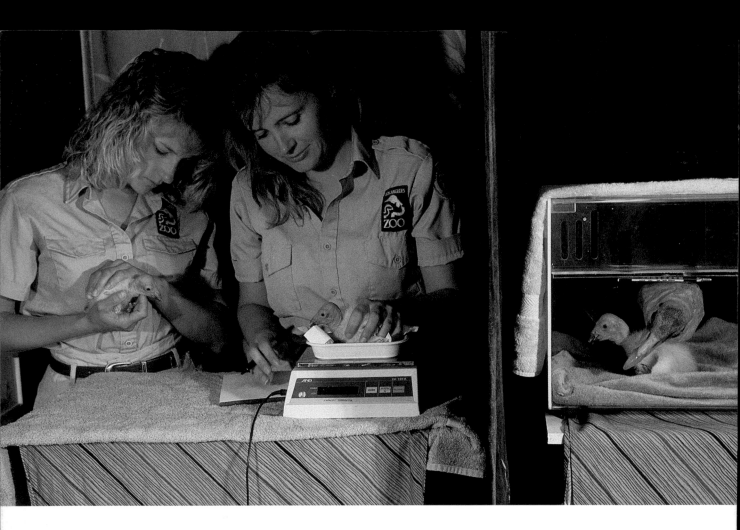

IN THE WILD, the condor parents take turns searching for food. The adult bird eats the food and stores it in a pouch in its neck called a crop. Up to three pounds of food can be stored there at one time! When the parent condor returns to the nest, the hungry chick flaps its wings and the two birds touch beaks. The parent then regurgitates, or coughs up, the food for the chick to eat. A young chick is fed about sixteen times a week, or about twice a day. As the chick grows older, it eats more, but less often.

ABOVE: *Keepers weigh the birds regularly to check their growth.*

RIGHT: *A condor chick touches beaks with its puppet parent.*

At the zoo, the chicks are fed pieces of cut-up mice. Although the keepers feed the chicks directly at first, the young birds must not get used to seeing people. By the chick's second or third day, all of its feedings are with condor-shaped puppets. The keeper stays behind a curtain so the chick only sees the condor puppet bringing food in its beak. This fools the young bird into believing it is being fed by its parents. Reducing human contact helps captive-bred birds adjust more easily to life in the wild when they are released.

A YOUNG CONDOR CHICK grows rapidly, and by the time it is three months old, its down begins to be replaced by dark feathers. It starts to hop around the nest area and flap its wings but does not practice flying in a serious way until its feathers are complete. This usually happens when it is about six months old. The bird is then about the same size as an adult. The dark gray-green skin on the head and neck of a young bird gradually changes color as it progresses toward adulthood. It achieves its full adult coloring and ability to breed when it is about six years old.

BETWEEN 1986 AND 1991, the captive breeding programs in Los Angeles and San Diego progressed faster than anyone had predicted. In 1989 four chicks hatched; in 1990, eight; and in 1991, there were twelve more, bringing the total population to fifty-two. In four years of captive breeding the number of condors had nearly doubled! Sooner than had been expected, there were enough condors to begin returning some of them to the wild.

To practice the techniques necessary to make reintroduction a success, scientists in California had experimented earlier with a group of puppet-reared female Andean condor chicks. The first problem had been to find a suitable place to release the young birds. They chose a cliff in a remote canyon near the Sespe Condor Sanctuary. This area, located in the Los Padres National Forest, just north of Los Angeles, is part of the traditional California condor range. Hunting is forbidden there, and the area is protected from outside disturbances. It also contains numerous nest sites, which would later be useful for California condors.

At the release site, a passageway allowed caretakers to give food to the chicks without being seen, and blinds were built so that observers could monitor the birds before and after their release. Electric fences around the release site helped to keep out bears that might be drawn to the condors' food. At first, a net over the pen portion of the release site prevented the chicks from leaving. Then, when the chicks were seven months old, the net was removed and the young Andean condors were free to make their first attempts at flying.

TOP: *From their enclosure, the young Andean condors can see the landscape below.*

BOTTOM: *The Andean condors practice flying in California.*

WHEN A YOUNG BIRD leaves its nest for the first time, it has fledged. In the wild, a fledged condor perches on rocks and branches near the nest site while it waits for its parents to bring food. Each day, the youngster takes short trial flights and gradually becomes more skilled at flying. Several months later, the young condor is able to fly with the adults as they search for food and water. It will then start to feed itself, though its parents may also continue to feed it for a time.

The young Andean condors in California soon began flying longer distances from the feeding platform and eventually were exploring many miles away. Each bird wore solar- and battery-powered radio transmitters on its wings. The scientists followed the birds' movements by listening to the beeps of the transmitters on a radio receiver. Although the Andean condors sometimes flew far away, they learned to return to the sanctuary for food.

Even after California condors are reestablished in the wild, wildlife managers will continue to feed them for some time. This will encourage the birds to stay within the sanctuary and help prevent them from eating carcasses elsewhere that might contain lead bullets.

Of the thirteen Andean condors released in the Los Padres National Forest, twelve survived. (One, inexperienced at flying, died when it crashed into power lines.) The birds proved that, with help, condors could thrive again in southern California. When the Andean condors' part of the program was finished, they were recaptured and taken to South America, where they were released permanently into their native environment.

Two young Andean condors spread their wings.

36

ON OCTOBER 10, 1991, the first California condors were taken back to the wild. They were Xewe (*gay-wee*), a female hatched at the Los Angeles Zoo on April 8, 1991, and Chocuyens, (*cho-koo-yenz*) a male hatched at the San Diego Wild Animal Park on May 29, 1991. In the Chumash language, Xewe means "to cast a shadow" and Chocuyens means "valley of the moon."

Xewe and Chocuyens, accompanied by two Andean condors, were loaded into cloth-covered crates and flown by helicopter from Los Angeles to the release site. There they were placed inside an enclosed roost box that opened to an outside net-covered pen. Caretakers from the U.S. Fish and Wildlife Service hid in a blind behind the roost box and continued to feed the chicks just as they had been fed at the zoo. (In several years, before the Andean condors reach breeding age, they will be captured so they do not mate with the California birds.)

LEFT: *The condor chicks were transported in sturdy carriers to the release site.*

ABOVE: *Buildings at the release site, hidden behind protective fences, blend into the natural environment.*

RIGHT: *Xewe waits inside the release pen for her chance to be free.*

As with the Andean condors that previously had been released, the California condor chicks and their Andean companions were prevented from leaving their pen at first. But on January 14, 1992, many people, including scientists, reporters, and representatives from several Native American tribes, watched as the young birds left their pen and flew without any restrictions. After 5½ years in captivity, California condors were free again!

LEFT: *The young condors learn to return to the release site for food — in this case, a stillborn calf.*

ABOVE: *Wearing a costume made of feathers, a member of the Chumash tribe does a traditional condor dance. The Chumash believe that if all the condors die, so will their tribe.*

DURING THE FIRST WEEKS after Chocuyens and Xewe were released, they took only short flights, but as their confidence increased they spent more and more time in the air. Like other soaring birds, a condor flies mainly by catching rising air currents called thermals, or wind deflected off cliff faces. Circling with the upwardly moving air, condors can easily climb to heights of thousands of feet.

The long, strong flight feathers on the ends of the wings are called primaries. The condor can tip and control each of these almost as if it were a tiny wing, which allows the condor to carefully position itself in rising air and soar upward. The condor can also use its tail to steer or to brake when coming in to land.

When a condor soars, the primary feathers at its wingtips are extended.

Gliding condors have been timed at speeds of 55 MPH in straight flight and may be able to fly as fast as 100 MPH. In the right air conditions, a condor is capable of climbing above 15,000 feet. Normally, though, a condor will rise to between 3,000 and 6,000 feet before beginning a long gliding flight to the next thermal.

Condors are among the most accomplished of the soaring birds, with bodies superbly designed to keep them airborne for long periods of time. Once aloft, the large size of the condor provides considerable momentum, and its lightweight, compact wings give the bird strength and maneuverability.

In flight, a bird can change the shape of its wings by expanding or folding its feathers. At rest, the feathers lie flat and smooth.

WITH LUCK AND GOOD MANAGEMENT, more young California condors will join Xewe and Chocuyens in years to come, and they will all grow up, mate, and produce chicks for many years. California condors are long-lived, and in zoos they have been known to reach the age of forty.

As the number of condors increases, additional breeding facilities will be built at other zoos. And as more birds hatch in captivity and become available for release, more release sites will be built. Over time, scientists hope to establish two independent groups of wild condors with about one hundred and fifty birds in each group.

It will be many years before we know if the California condor will be able to survive on its own in the wild. For most people, seeing a wild California condor will always be a rare and thrilling experience. However, as the condors become reestablished in the wild and their numbers increase in captivity, some will be returned to public exhibits in zoos so that people can get to know them up close.

Every living thing interacts with other species that share the same environment. If one species disappears, it changes the balance of life in that ecosystem. As land is set aside where condors can live safely, other species that share the same habitat are protected as well. An important additional benefit of the California Condor Recovery Program is that new techniques are being developed that can be used to help save endangered birds all over the world.

A wild condor nests in a giant sequoia tree.

THE CONDOR IS an impressive creature that dominated the skies forty thousand years ago when mammoths roamed the earth. But unlike mammoths, which are now extinct, the condor is still with us. Its life is a link to the past as well as a lesson for the future. The condor is just one of many species whose existence has been threatened by people's carelessness and ignorance. Although the battle to save the California condor is not yet over, the number of birds increases each year, and the outlook is hopeful. By the end of the 1992 breeding season, another twelve condor chicks had hatched, bringing the total number of birds to sixty-four. The California condor still teeters on the brink of extinction, but with luck and the continued hard work of many devoted people, it may once again grace the skies of western North America.

The California condor

Index